NATURE
In Your
BACKYARD
Simple Activities for Children

By Susan Lang

WITH THE STAFF OF CAYUGA NATURE CENTER

Illustrated by Sharon Lane Holm

The Millbrook Press
Brookfield, Connecticut

Thanks go to the educators at Cayuga Nature Center
for their contributions to this book.

Library of Congress Cataloging-in-Publication Data
Lang, Susan S.
Nature in your backyard: simple activities for children / by Susan S. Lang
with the staff of Cayuga Nature Center; illustrated by Sharon Lane Holm.
Summary: Through a series of projects, experiments, and activities that
are simple enough for young children to do, this illustrated book presents
the natural world that's right outside the door.
p. cm.
Includes bibliographical references (p.   ) and index.
ISBN 1-56294-451-7 (lib. bdg.) ISBN 1-56294-893-8 (pbk.)
1. Nature study–Activity programs–Juvenile literature. [1. Nature study.]
I. Holm, Sharon Lane, ill. II. Cayuga Nature Center (Ithaca, N.Y.) III. Title.
QH54.5.L36 1995
508–dc20   94-9278 CIP AC

Published by The Millbrook Press
2 Old New Milford Road
Brookfield, Connecticut 06804

For Julia and all her friends at the Caroline Elementary School (Ithaca, New York), especially Paulette Conroy, Sue Eslinger, Geeta Jain, Ann Jankey, and Deby Ward for their teaching gifts and the love of learning they inspire.

Susan S. Lang

For all those curious naturalists who visit Cayuga Nature Center and inspire the staff to explore with them the wonders of the natural world.

Dick Taylor for Cayuga Nature Center

For Michael

Sharon Lane Holm

A Note for Preserving Nature

Whenever possible, try to enjoy and not disturb nests, plants, or animals out in the woods or fields:

When you do collect any plants, seeds, and flowers, take just a few of a kind, making sure there are plenty left.

If you are catching insects or other critters, be gentle, and let them loose after you are done with the project.

Do not bother birds that are nesting or feeding, and do not touch or steal birds' eggs.

Pick up any garbage you see, and don't leave any yourself!

Contents

1 Insects and Worms

Miss Ant: Don't Find Us—
We'll Find You!

Do this activity on a warm, dry day.

You need:

a slice of bread, cut up into
    small pieces (no bigger
    than chocolate chips)
a cup of water
2 teaspoons sugar
paper and pencil

What to do:

Put the sugar in the water and mix until dissolved. Soak the
bread in the sugar water for at least ten seconds.

Place five pieces together in one spot in the yard. Draw a
map to show where you put them. Place another five crumbs
somewhere else. Show on the map where you put them.
Continue until all your bread is gone.

Check the bread spots every half hour to see how long it
takes for ants to find the bread.
Keep checking to see how long
it takes for the bread to be
carried away.

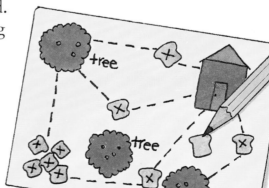

What happens:

Can you find all the pieces you put out? Are there any ants near the pieces? Do they break off small pieces of the bread to carry, or do they work together to drag big pieces back to the nest? Can you follow the ants carrying the pieces? Can you find their nest?

Why:

Worker ants, which are females, are always on the lookout for food. They will probably find the pieces of bread and try to carry them back to their nest. Chances are, they smelled the food with their antennae before they saw it. Although other animals (a dog, a cat, wild birds) may find the bread, look closely to see if ants have been attracted also—you'll see many of them around each piece they have found.

Even if an ant sees food, it won't pick the food up unless it can smell with its antennae that it *is* food.

Amazing Ants

Ants are amazing insects. They are one of the most common insects and live in nearly every part of the world. There are thousands of different species (kinds) of ants.

While the worker ants are always female and the ones out looking for food, the males live only for a few weeks, long enough to mate with the huge queen so she can lay eggs.

Ants eat many things. Some eat seeds, some eat plant juices, some eat fungi, and some even eat other insects!

Excuse Me, Miss Ant

You need:

a grassy lawn in spring, summer,
  or fall
two pencils

What to do:

Find an ant trail by either using
the activity on page 6 or finding
an ant nest. (Some nests are
under anthills, which are the
entrance tunnels to the nests.
Other nests are under rocks and
logs.) If you find a nest, be
careful not to hurt the ants.

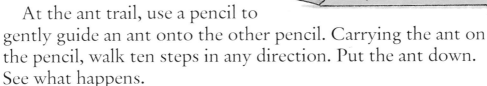

   At the ant trail, use a pencil to
gently guide an ant onto the other pencil. Carrying the ant on
the pencil, walk ten steps in any direction. Put the ant down.
See what happens.

What happens:

Did your ant find its way back to the trail? Did it go directly
or seem lost for a while? How long did it take? Did it go back
to its nest or to food?

Why:

The ant will almost always find her way back to her trail because when most common ants leave their nests, they mark their trails with a scent. Other ants from the same nest use their sense of smell to follow the trails. The trails help them to find their way to food that has been discovered and also to find their way back to the nest. If moved off the trail, the ants will use their antennae to get back to the trail and either continue to search for food or go back to the nest.

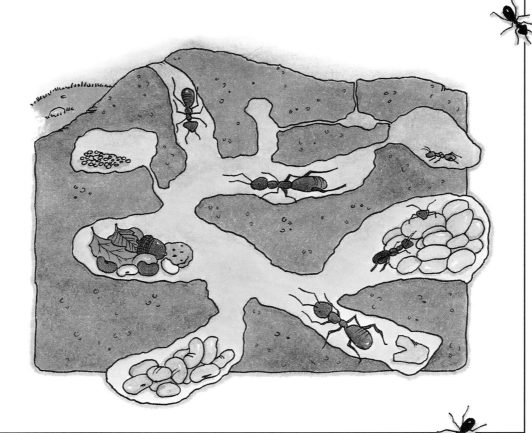

A Bottle of Bugs

You need:

a large (2-liter) plastic
   soda bottle
a cup
a shoebox
soil from a yard

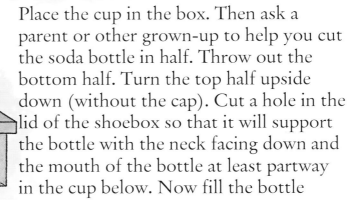

What to do:

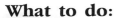

Place the cup in the box. Then ask a parent or other grown-up to help you cut the soda bottle in half. Throw out the bottom half. Turn the top half upside down (without the cap). Cut a hole in the lid of the shoebox so that it will support the bottle with the neck facing down and the mouth of the bottle at least partway in the cup below. Now fill the bottle (with the spout facing down) half way with the soil. Put the entire setup under a desk lamp that is close enough to warm the soil. See what happens.

What happens:

After an hour or so, look inside the cup and box. Are there any insects in there? Where did they come from? How many different kinds do you see? Why do you think they went into the cup?

Why:

Soil is home to many things, including insects, eggs, seeds, and other living things too small to see without a microscope. As the soil warms up from the heat of the lamp, insects and other little crawly creatures, most of which are sensitive to heat, feel it and will travel away from it until they fall out the mouth of the bottle.

Billions and Billions of Bugs

Here, there, everywhere, there are bugs. If you measured off a section of air 1 mile (1.6 kilometers) on each side, you would find some 25 billion insects—and that doesn't count all the bugs that are within 50 feet (15 meters) of the ground. (A billion is one thousand millions. Or, put differently, if you had a billion dollars and spent a dollar every minute, it would take almost two thousand years to spend!) In just a cubic yard of dirt (about a bathtub full), there are anywhere from five hundred to two thousand insects. In one moist football field, there might be some four million insects. (Dry fields wouldn't support insect life as well.)

And there are so many kinds of insects, too. In fact, there are more than four times as many kinds of insects as there are other kinds of animals.

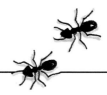

Getting Worms to Eat Your Garbage

You need:

a cardboard shoebox (as large
   as possible)
a recycled plastic bag to line
   the box
newspaper or old
   damp leaves
vegetable scraps from the kitchen
garden soil
about 150 red worms ("red wrigglers") from
   a bait shop, or as many worms from someone's
   compost pile
a full cup of water

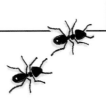

What to do:

Line the inside of the shoebox with
the plastic. Carefully poke four
or five holes in each side of the
box and plastic lining. Rip
twelve to fifteen pages of
newspaper into strips about
2 inches (5 centimeters) wide.
Fill the box half full with the
strips of newspaper (or the
old leaves). Sprinkle half of the cup of water
and two handfuls of garden soil onto the bedding.

Fill the box with the rest of the newspaper strips (or old leaves) and add the rest of the water and two more handfuls of soil. Everything should be damp, though not wet. Mix the bedding with your hands. Add more water if it is not moist. Put the worms in the box and cover it.

Each day, mix two or three tablespoons of kitchen scraps into the bedding—vegetable peels, coffee grounds, eggshells, stale bread, and leftovers, but no meat or dairy products. Add enough water each day to keep the bedding moist. Over time, if you notice the newspaper and leaves are almost gone, add more soil and newspaper.

What happens:

Watch what happens to the kitchen scraps in the box. Do you notice any changes in the soil, leaves, and shredded newspaper that you put into the box? What do you think the worms do?

Why:

If you have enough worms, they will eat most of the kitchen scraps. The food eaten by the worms gets broken up into tiny little pieces that will be excreted, or passed out, by the worms as "castings"—crumbly bits of new rich soil. The castings can be removed and will make wonderful garden soil.

Worms also improve the soil by burrowing through the dirt, making lots of holes that help the soil hold air and water. But it is the waste that the worms produce after eating the vegetable garbage and leaves that makes the soil so rich.

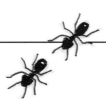

2 Birds

Best Nest Builders

You need:

a collection of things
    that birds use to
    build nests, such as
    twigs, sticks, dirt, hair, old
    spider webs, feathers, moss, grasses,
    leaves, pine needles, bark, milkweed
    or dandelion fuzz, cottontails, thread,
    strings, bits of plastic, and the like
a bowl of dirt
a cup of water
a spoon or two popsicle sticks
newspaper or cardboard to work on

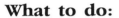

What to do:

First, mix the dirt and water until you have a bowl of mud that is about as thick as mashed potatoes. Then, try to make a nest as neatly as possible, with a smooth lining of mud on the inside, just like a robin's nest. If you want an extra challenge, pretend you're doing the job as a bird does with its beak. Use only two popsicle sticks (and not your fingers) for your "beak."

What happens:

How hard is it to make a nest? Compare your nest with a nest actually made by a bird (but don't move the bird's nest, because some birds will reuse old nests the next year).

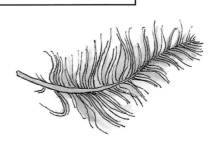

Why:

Weaving sticks, hair, threads, and other small objects together is a tricky job, especially if you have to do it with your beak!

Nests: From Practically Nothing to Natural Wonders

Most birds will build nests to hold their eggs and protect their young (nests are not "homes" for the adults). But nests vary as much as birds do.

Killdeers, for example, scrape the ground a little and may line the shallow scraping with pebbles and grass. Many waterbirds also lay their eggs on a few pebbles or pieces of grass along the shore.

Tree nests, though, have to be strong so that rain and wind won't ruin them. Robins' nests always look very well made because these birds "glue" their nests together with mud to make very smooth linings. Orioles build pouches that hang from trees.

Chimney swifts build nests shaped like saucers and glued together by bird saliva into chimneys or hollow trees. Other birds make nests on piles of mud, in dead tree trunks, in caves, and on leaves.

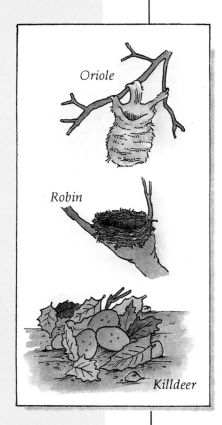

Oriole

Robin

Killdeer

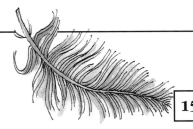

What Do Birds Like for Their Nests?

You need:

3 pinecones (or hairbrushes)

yarn: 5 pieces of 4 different
    colors, cut into short and
    long lengths (6 inches and
    9 inches, or 15 and 23
    centimeters)

5 thin paper strips of several colors, at least as long as the yarn

5 cloth strips, about the same sizes

5 pieces of string, about the same sizes

other items that a bird might want for a nest, such as plastic
    straws or other plastic items, hair from a hairbrush,
    cottonballs, and the like

one longer piece of yarn or string

What to do:

Tie the longer piece of string around the tops of the pinecones
(or brushes) so they hang from the string.

    Make a list of how many pieces you have of different
colored yarns, cloth, string, and paper strips and other
materials. Then stick the materials between the scales of the
pinecones tightly enough that they don't fall out but not so
tightly that they can't be easily pulled out. Hang the pinecones
outside a window in the late winter or early spring. Each week,
figure out what's missing.

What happens:

Birds will come and take away the materials for their nests. Which materials went first? What colors attracted the birds the most? Did they like the earthen colors such as green, tan, and brown or bright colors like red and purple?

Why:

Different kinds of birds like to build their nests from different things. Red-winged blackbirds, for example, like to use cattail fluff and leaves. Robins use small sticks and mud. Tiny ruby-throated hummingbirds like to use moss and lichen. Scientists who study birds, called ornithologists, have found all kinds of shiny man-made objects in the nests of crows, including a wristwatch. In other kinds of nests, ornithologists have found horsehair, snakeskins, and pieces of bark.

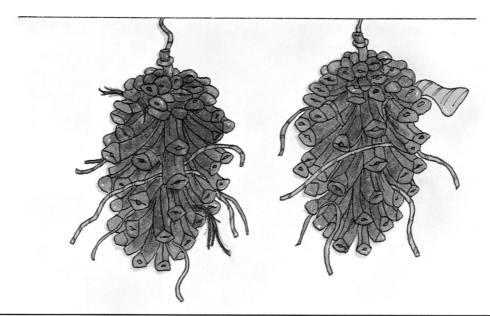

Making a Bird Feeder from Recycled Materials

You need:

a cardboard milk carton
birdseed
string or rope
a paper clip

What to do:

Wash the milk carton out and staple the top opening closed. Cut an opening as shown, holding the front flap open with a paper clip (the clip holds the door flap up to form a little roof over the doorway). Attach string (or wire) through a hole punched in the top edge to hang the feeder from a branch. Cut a few small drainage holes in the carton's bottom. Hang the carton and fill it with seed.

Using several bird feeders, try putting different seeds in each one and see which your visiting birds like. You might even try to collect some wild seeds and see if the birds like them.

What happens:

How many different kinds of birds come? Does the kind of birdseed you put out make a difference?

Why:

You will attract the birds in your region that eat seeds. Depending on the kind of birdseed you put out, different kinds of birds will come. Birds will choose the seeds that give them the most energy.

Although birds can find wild seeds by themselves, they love to visit bird feeders because it makes their lives easier, especially in cold weather. In the winter, the birds that visit feeders may come to depend upon the food, so keep feeding them all winter.

Extra activity:
Charting your visitors

Try putting up three feeders. Fill each with different kinds of seeds (such as sunflower, millet, cracked corn). Watch to see which birds visit each day for a week. Make a chart to record your observations. If you don't know the names of the birds that visit, make up a name that describes it, such as "The Red Bird" or "The Big Red Racer" for a very red bird (a cardinal) or "The Noisy Blue Bird" or "The Big Blue Bomber" for a bird with a lot of blue (a blue jay). Later, you can get a guide book from the library to identify the birds.

Number of times I saw these birds eat

Feeder	Cardinal or Red Racer	Blue Jay or Blue Bomber	Red Winged Blackbird
Sunflower #1	‖‖	‖‖ ‖‖	II
Millet Seed #2	I	II	
Cracked Corn #3		I	III

How to Sneak Up on a Bird

You need:

any kind of bird feeder, next to a window
a shipping box smaller than the window
wide shipping tape
enough dark paper, newspaper, or cardboard
    to cover up the rest of the window

What to do:

With the help of a grown-up, cut the top of the box off, and cut a slit in the bottom of the box that is about as wide and long as a pencil. If more than one person is going to spy at a time, cut slits on the sides of the box also. These slits should be side to side (horizontal), not up and down (vertical).

Tape the box to the window so the slit is lined up with the bird feeder. Cover the rest of the window with the dark paper or cardboard. Spy all you want.

What happens:

What usually happens when you go near a window where a bird is at a feeder? Does the bird blind make a difference?

Why:

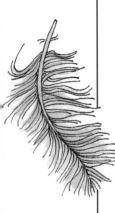

Birds can see (and hear) very, very well. They will notice the slightest movement right away. If you cover the window and peek out through very small slits, birds won't fly away as they usually do when people get close to a window to view them. You can sneak all the peeks you want.

Be a Human Scarecrow and Attract Birds

You need:

old clothes, including a hat,
   gloves, raincoat, pants
a tray
birdseed
an outdoor chair

What to do:

Make a scarecrow by stuffing the clothes with straw, hay, or crumpled newspaper. Sit the scarecrow on the chair with its hands in its lap, and place the tray on top of them. Keep birdseed in the tray and on the scarecrow's hat and hands.

    After a few weeks, put on clothes like the scarecrow's. Wear the scarecrow's hat and gloves, put the scarecrow out of view, and sit in the chair. Put birdseed on your hat and hold the tray of birdseed. Sit perfectly still for at least fifteen minutes. Then put the scarecrow back and try again the next day.

What happens:

How long does it take for birds to approach you?

Why:

Scarecrows are usually made to scare birds away, but birds will get used to yours and discover they won't be harmed by taking some seeds from it. The birds will begin to ignore the scarecrow. Later, when you take the scarecrow's place, they will learn to ignore you.

3 Backyard Animals

Keeping Snug in Winter

You need:

a day outside with snow on the
    ground; the outside temperature
    should be at least 41°F (50°C) or less.
a box of gelatin (or gelatin
    dessert mix)
4 small containers the same size,
    such as film, pill, or spice
    containers, small paper cups, or
    plastic popsicle makers (use
    plastic wrap and rubber bands to
    make tops if the containers don't have them)
a large spoon, small shovel, or trowel

What to do:

First, find three different places near your house where an
animal might hide in the winter to stay warm (for example,
under snow, under a log, under a pile of leaves). Ask a
grown-up to help you heat the gelatin and water on the
stove, according to the package's directions.

Fill each identical cup or container about three-quarters
full with the liquid gelatin. Cover.

Put a cup in each of the three places you've picked. Put the
fourth one outside in the open.

Check the four cups every five minutes to see which gets
hard first, second, third, and fourth.

What happens:

Knowing which container hardened first and which hardened last, can you figure out which is the warmest spot? The coldest? Is it warmest under the leaves? Under snow? In a sunny spot?

Why:

The gelatin in the coldest place will get hard first. The one in the warmest spot will harden last. Snow and leaves are good insulators, like the warm covers on your bed—they can keep an animal warmer than it would be out in the open air. That's why most animals in the winter find a cozy nook under leaves or even snow to stay warm. What do you think would happen if they stayed out in the open?

Deep Freeze: Frogs Under the Mud

In the colder regions of the world, frogs spend winter in a sleeplike state. They do not eat or drink all winter. But they must find a place where they will not freeze or get too dry. In late fall bullfrogs, for example, dig into the soft mud at the bottom of a pond. Under the deep water, the mud does not freeze. There the frog can remain all winter safely. In spring, when the air warms up, the frog digs out—and is it hungry!

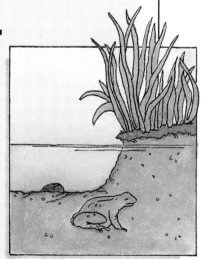

Footprint Fun

You need:

a large baking tray or
    cardboard box that
      has been cut so the sides
      are only 1 inch (2.5 centi-
      meters) high
sand, dirt, or flour
cookie, peanut butter on a
    cracker, or other food that you
    think an animal would like

What to do:

Take everything to an open garage, back porch, driveway, or sidewalk. Fill the box with the sand, dirt, or flour (not a mix of them) and smooth it out. If using dirt or sand, make it wet enough so that the impression of a handprint would remain if a hand were pressed into it. Put the food in the middle of the box on top of the sand, dirt, or flour.

Leave the box out overnight. In the morning, check to see if the food is gone and if an animal has left tracks. The tracks may be in the box or around it.

What happens:

Did an animal come to take the food during the night? How can you tell? Can you identify the tracks of the animal? What came—squirrel, bird, mouse? Use the chart to help you. Can you draw the shape of the tracks you saw?

Why:

Animals will be drawn to the box by the food, which they can smell for some distance. Each kind of animal has a different footprint. If we study animal tracks, we can learn not only what animal made them but even what the animal was doing (running, hopping, or chasing another animal, for example).

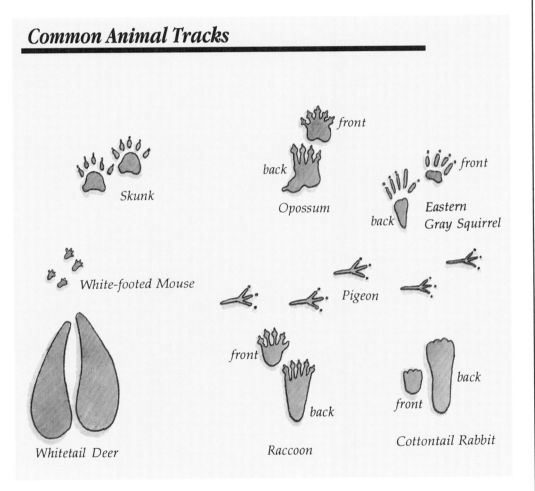

Common Animal Tracks

Skunk

Opossum
front
back

Eastern Gray Squirrel
front
back

White-footed Mouse

Pigeon

Whitetail Deer

Raccoon
front
back

Cottontail Rabbit
back
front

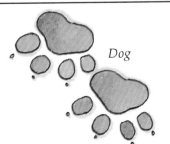

Dog

4 Seeds

Popcorn Crackling Trick

You need:

a cup of popcorn kernels
an aluminum pie pan
   (or a metal cookie sheet)
water

What to do:

Fill a cup to the top with popcorn kernels. Then add as much water as possible, and set the cup on the pan or cookie sheet. If you want to surprise someone (or even yourself!) slide the pan under a bed and leave it out of sight.

What happens:

In five or six hours, you will hear mysterious noises.

Why:

As the water gets into the seeds, they swell. Soon, so many have swollen that they don't fit in the cup anymore and tumble out, making a noise as they fall on the cookie sheet.

That's what happens in the soil. Seeds have hard, dry coverings called seed coats. Inside is all the important information a plant needs to grow. Seeds are like sleeping plants. They won't "wake up" until there is enough water to make the seed swell. This makes the seed coat burst open. Once the hard cover is broken, the seed inside will grow into a baby plant.

Which Way Is Up? Seeds Know!

You need:

a package of seeds (beans work best
  because they grow fast and are big,
  but any kind of large garden seed
  is okay)
a clear drinking glass or jar (use a
  rubber band and plastic wrap to
  make a lid for a drinking glass)
enough garden dirt or planting soil
  to fill the jar or glass
black paper
cellophane tape

What to do:

Fill the jar with dirt, but not to the very top. Moisten the dirt
with water.

Push a seed down along the side of the jar into the soil, as
far as about two knuckles on your index finger. Do the same
thing with three more seeds around the side of the jar.

Wrap the jar with black paper, taping it or using paper clips
to keep it in place.

Check the seeds every day by loosening the paper and
looking to see if they have started to sprout. Check the dirt
for moisture, and water if dry. Reattach the paper after
checking.

After the seeds sprout and the sprouts are about 1/2 inch
(12 millimeters) long, put the jar on its side. Wait a few days.

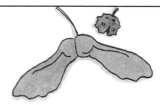

After the sprouts grow some more, put the lid on the jar (or cover the glass with the plastic wrap and a rubber band) and turn the jar upside down.

What happens:

In what direction do the seeds grow? As you turn the jar, does the stem continue growing in the same direction or does it change? Does the stem remain straight? In what shape does the sprout grow after you've turned the jar several times?

Why:

No matter what direction you place the jar, the plant shoots will always try to grow up and the roots will always try to grow down toward the earth. As the jar is turned every few days, the sprout will take on a funny shape as it tries to keep growing upward. If you keep changing the direction of the jar, you might get the sprouts to grow in a circle.

Whenever you stop turning the jar, place it upright and remove the lid. The sprouts will eventually break through the soil and grow up, up, up. How does the plant know which way is up? The Earth's gravity pulls on the roots to grow into the soil (downward), while the stem grows in the opposite direction (up). Once the sprout breaks through the soil, it will then grow toward the sun.

Cover jar with black paper

Day 1,2,3

Day 4,5,6

Day 7,8,9

Day 10,11,12

Day 13,14,15

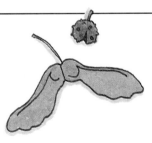

Hitchhiking Seeds

You need:

a sock big enough to put
    over your shoe
a piece of paper
an egg carton
a magnifying glass

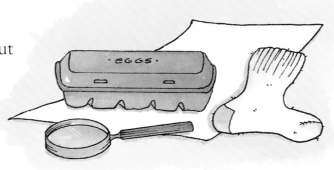

What to do:

Do this activity in summer or fall. Put the sock over your shoe; if it doesn't fit, you can tie it around your ankle. For about five minutes, walk, jump, and skip through high grass or bushes. Take the sock off and shake it over a piece of paper to collect anything that falls off. Pick out all the seeds on the paper and any that remain on the sock. Sort them, putting matching seeds together in the same cups of the egg carton. Look at each type of seed under the magnifying glass.

What happens:

Did many seeds fall? Why do some stick to the sock? How do you think that helps the plant?

Why:

Seeds stick to the sock because they are designed to "travel" and get away from the parent plant. Can you figure out how each type of seed travels? Look at the next page for some ideas.

Extra activities:

Drop a seed in front of a blowing fan and see how far it travels. That's how the seed would travel in the wind. Which seeds travel farthest?

Put the seeds in a box filled with about 2 inches (5 centimeters) of soil; sprinkle soil over them. Put them near a window and keep them moist, and see what grows.

Why Seeds Leave Home

By far, seeds are the most important parts of a plant because they contain all the information needed to grow new plants. But if seeds just dropped to the ground and grew, they would have to "fight" with their parents for water, light, and minerals in the soil. So seeds have to find ways to get away from home, and different seeds have developed different ways. Some "hitchhike" by being sticky or prickly and attaching to birds, animal fur, or people on their way. Others are eaten with their fruit by birds. The seeds pass through the bird's body and are dropped somewhere else where they may grow into new plants.

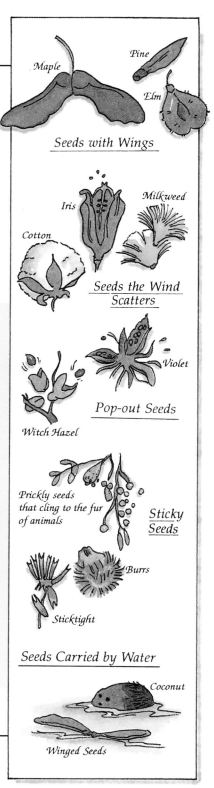

Seeds with Wings

Seeds the Wind Scatters

Pop-out Seeds

Sticky Seeds

Seeds Carried by Water

Winged Seeds

5 Plant Magic

Making Plants Stretch Toward the Light

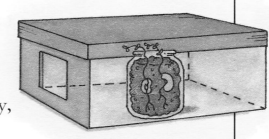

You need:

a shoebox (or another box that
  has a cover)
a jar or glass filled with dirt
a sprout from "Seeds Know!" activity,
  or a seed to start a sprout

What to do:

If starting with a seed, plant the seed in the jar of dirt. Water it every other day and once it has started growing, go to the next step.

   Cut a hole in one end of the box, either in the side or in the top of the box.

   Put the jar with the sprouted seed in the other side of the box.

   Put the box in a sunny place so the sun shines into the hole.

   Water the plant every other day by taking the box top off, but put the top back on after you've watered it.

What happens:

Which direction does the plant grow? Up? Down? Toward the hole? Why?

Why:

No matter where the hole is, green plants will grow toward the light because they need the sunlight's energy to make their own food. That's why they will try to grow where they get the best sunlight.

Extra activity:

After the plant starts growing toward the hole, try closing that hole and cutting a new one, and watch the plant grow toward it. You can make the plant grow in funny shapes by changing where the hole is every four or five days.

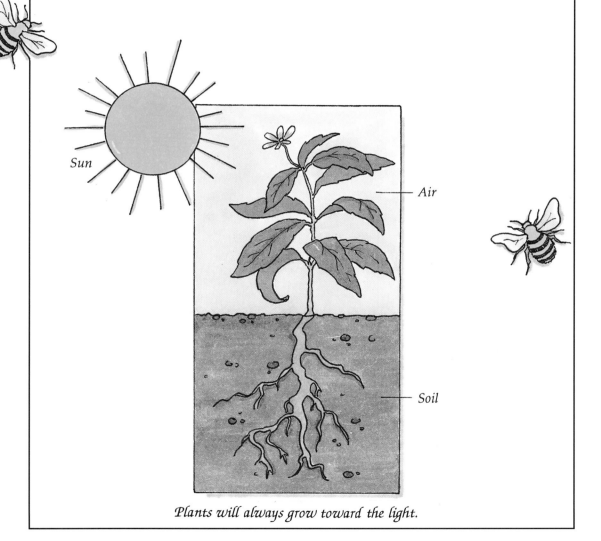

Sun

Air

Soil

Plants will always grow toward the light.

Sunshine to Greenshine

Do this activity in summer.

You need:

a mowed lawn
a garbage can cover or wooden
    board (any size larger than
    a shoebox)

What to do:

Place the garbage can cover or board
on the lawn so that all the grass under
it is well covered. (Ask a grown-up
to suggest a good out-of-the-way
place for this activity.) If the garbage
can cover is lightweight, put several rocks on it to hold it
down. Look under the cover or board in three days, then seven
days, and then in fourteen days. Remove it after two weeks.

What happens:

Is the grass a different color under the cover? Why? What do
you think would happen if you kept the cover on longer?

Why:

Plants are green because they contain a green substance called
chlorophyll, which the plant uses to make its own food.
Without the sun, new chlorophyll can't be made, and the
plant's supply is used up. That's why the grass under the cover

or board has become lighter green or even yellow. You can probably even see the shape of the garbage can cover or board on the grass.

This experiment shows you how sunshine helps make the green chlorophyll in plants. The chlorophyll then makes food for the plant. Many of those plants are food for us!

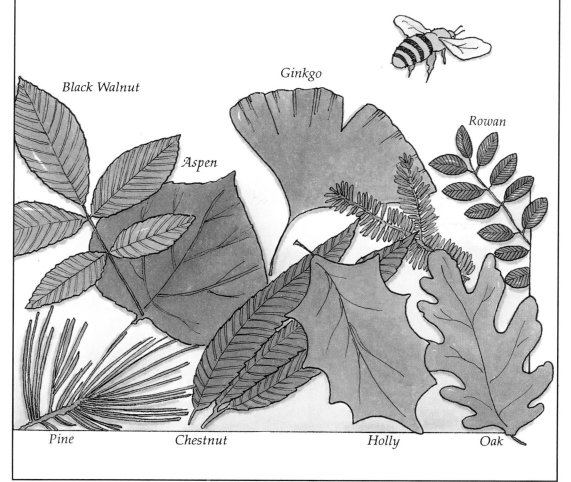

Black Walnut

Ginkgo

Rowan

Aspen

Pine

Chestnut

Holly

Oak

What Do Plants Need? Air

You need:

petroleum jelly

a tree or bush with green leaves, or a
    houseplant with green leaves (be
    sure you have permission to do this
    experiment on a houseplant)

What to do:

Spread a little petroleum jelly on the bottom
of one leaf, covering an area about the size of a
quarter. Spread the jelly all over the top and bottom of a
second leaf. See what happens in three days, in a week, and in
two weeks.

What happens:

Do the leaves change color? Which one changed more? Can
you figure out why?

Why:

The petroleum jelly blocks tiny airholes (called stomata) in the
leaves. Through these holes, plants exchange the gas oxygen
for carbon dioxide (the same gas that people and animals
breathe out). Without these gases the leaf dies, first turning
yellow. Eventually, it will turn brown and fall off. Some leaves
have stomata just on the bottom, but some have stomata on
the top and bottom. A leaf with petroleum jelly on just the
bottom may stay healthy longer.

Plants use the carbon dioxide that humans and animals breathe out, and they are able to produce more oxygen than they use. This extra oxygen is available for all of us to breathe!

The Rain Forest Tragedy

The world's tropical rain forests—thick jungle forests—are chock full of plants. They are very helpful to the world environment because they use a lot of carbon dioxide, produce much of the world's.oxygen, and are homes for half the world's species (kinds) of plants and animals.

Rain forests are very important, but they are rapidly being destroyed. Every second, an area of rain forest about the size of a football field is cut down by people for farming, logging, and cattle ranching somewhere in the world. We need to protect these forests so the world's environment stays healthy.

Saving Summer's Beauty: Pressed Flower Note Cards

You need:

heavy paper for notecards, or white clothing cardboard (from pantyhose or laundered shirts)

a bouquet of wild or garden flowers that are small enough to fit on a postcard, or on a quarter of your paper

paper towels

glue, cellophane tape, or clear adhesive plastic

What to do:

Lay the flowers gently on top of two layers of paper towel. Cover the flowers with two more layers of paper towel. Place under a large heavy book (a dictionary or large phone book will work), or several lighter books, or even a pile of magazines. Leave for at least several days (a week in damp or humid weather) until they are dry.

Fold your paper in half and then fold it in half again to make a card. If you are using cardboard, cut it into the size of a postcard. Now glue a flower on your notecard or postcard. Another method is to place clear tape or clear adhesive plastic over the flower.

Write to a friend or relative!

What happens:

What do the paper towels and heavy book do to the flowers? Why does that make them last a longer time than usual?

Why:

Pressing the flowers between paper towels will squeeze the moisture (water) out of the flowers. Water helps to hold up plants and flowers. Usually, when plants dry out they droop (wilt) and fall apart. Pressing them, though, holds them in one position until they are dry and stiff.

6 Soil, Air, and Water

Grow a Dirt Garden

You need:

the top to a shoebox
a plastic bag cut flat to line the box top
dirt from three different places (for example, a garden,
    the middle of a yard, under a bush, the woods)

What to do:

On the boxtop, draw two lines so you have divided it into
three spaces. Extend the lines over the sides of the lid so you
can see them from the side.

Then line the boxtop with the plastic bag. Using the guides
on the sides of the box, fill each space with dirt from a
different place.

Keep soil moist, watering it perhaps every other day. Wait
to see what grows.

What happens:

Plants will grow! Can you figure out where they came from?

Why:

Dirt is made up of not only tiny pieces of rock and minerals but also many other things, such as seeds. When you keep the dirt moist, the seeds burst open and sprout. Count and see how many different kinds of plants grow in each square. Any difference?

Extra activity:

With a magnifying glass or microscope, examine some dirt. What do you see?

Growing a Garden on a Piece of Bread

You need:

3 pieces of white bread (the lighter the bread,
   the easier it will be to see what happens)
3 clean jars with tops (plastic or foil tops are fine)
a magnifying glass

What to do:

Touching only one corner, take one piece
of bread and put it immediately into one
jar. Cover the jar. Dampen the second piece
of bread by lightly sprinkling water onto
it with your fingers. Leave it outside for
twenty minutes; then put it in a jar and
cover. Dampen the third piece of bread also.
Then rub it with both palms of your hands and along a kitchen
counter. Put it in the third jar and cover. Label each jar. Put
the jars in a dark closet and check every three days.

What happens:

What do you see? Which bread has the most change? Examine
the bread with a magnifying glass.

Why:

Although you can't see them, air is loaded with spores—which
fungi and some plants use instead of seeds to reproduce—and
bacteria (tiny one-celled beings). The bread provides plenty of
food for the spores and bacteria to grow. The fuzzy growths

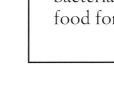

are spores, and the flat, wet growths are the bacteria. The bread rubbed along the kitchen counter has picked up the most spores and bacteria.

What's in Air?

Air looks invisible but it's got lots of stuff in it:

- *flakes of dead skin that fall off people every day*
- *dust from some faraway desert*
- *salt from a distant sea*
- *bits of insect legs, heads, and shells*
- *tiny chips of pavement and brick*
- *tiny eggs from insects and parasites*
- *fibers that have broken off clothing and furniture*

Most of these things don't hurt us. But sometimes people can put harmful chemicals into the air. Much of this air pollution is caused by cars and factories.

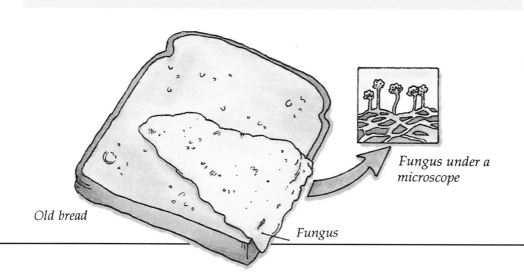

Fungus under a microscope

Old bread

Fungus

Making a Water Scope

You need:

a large tin can (a half-gallon size is perfect)
heavy clear plastic wrap (or large clear plastic bags)
2 to 3 large heavy rubber bands

What to do:

Ask a grown-up to remove the top and bottom
of the can and pound smooth any sharp edges
with a hammer or tape them with heavy tape.
Cut the plastic into pieces large enough to fit
over one end of the can with 2 inches (5 centimeters) overlapping on the sides. Secure with the
rubber bands. Kneel on the edge of a stream or pond and put
the covered end into the water. Look through the open end.

What happens:

Can you see beneath the surface of the water? What can you
find?

Why:

Without a scope, it's hard to see into
the water because of the reflections,
ripples, and the film that settles on
the surface. The scope lets you get
through the surface.

What's in Pond Water?

Although a small pond in the backyard may seem like a quiet little puddle of water, it is a very busy and active world for the creatures in it. A typical pond may have garter snakes, worms, minnows, sunfish, frogs, tadpoles, salamanders, turtles, clams, snakes, fisher spiders, crayfish, and all kinds of insects such as water bugs, water boatmen, water striders, dragonfly nymphs and mosquito and other insect larvae (young)—not to mention all the water plants!

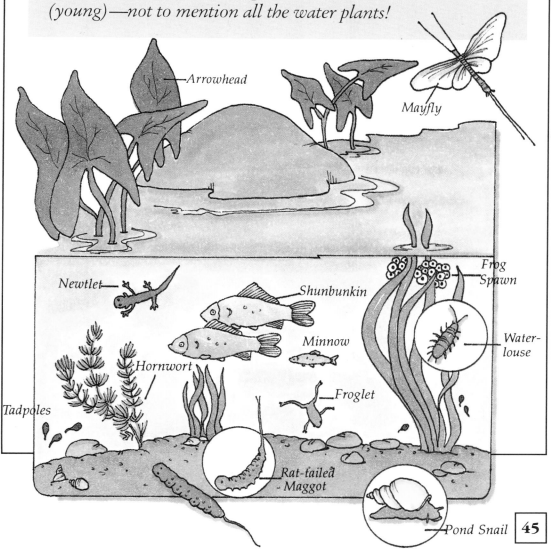

Arrowhead

Mayfly

Newtlet

Shunbunkin

Minnow

Frog Spawn

Water-louse

Tadpoles

Hornwort

Froglet

Rat-tailed Maggot

Pond Snail

Find Out More About Backyard Nature

Arnosky, Jim. *Crinkleroot's Book of Animal Tracking.* Macmillan, 1989.

Bowden, Marcia. *Nature for the Very Young: A Handbook of Indoor & Outdoor Activities.* John Wiley & Sons, 1989.

Braus, Judy. *Ranger Rick's Nature Scope: Incredible Insects.* National Wildlife Federation, 1986.

_____. *Ranger Rick's Nature Scope: Let's Hear It for Herps!* National Wildlife Federation, 1987.

Harlow, Rosie, and Gareth Morgan. *One Hundred Seventy-five Amazing Nature Experiments.* Random House, 1992.

Lavies, Bianca. *Compost Critters.* Dutton, 1993.

Markle, Sandra. *Outside and Inside Trees.* Bradbury Press. 1993.

Wilkes, Angels. *My First Nature Book.* Knopf, 1990.

Index

About the Author and Illustrator

Susan S. Lang is a senior science writer at Cornell University in Ithaca, New York. She is a former children's librarian and the author of seven other books and more than 125 articles for national magazines. This is her second children's book.

Cayuga Nature Center is a private, not-for-profit educational organization in Ithaca. Its programs include environmental education for area schools, nature day camps, seasonal festivals, and teacher-training workshops. The center's rustic lodge, with dormitories, kitchen, and dining areas, is set on 128 acres of woods, fields, streams, and ravines.

Sharon Lane Holm won awards for her work in advertising design before shifting her concentration to children's books. Her illustrations have since added zest to books for both the trade and educational markets. She lives in New Fairfield, Connecticut.